Earth-Friendly Wood Crafts in 5 Easy Steps

Anna Llimós

Enslow Elementary
an imprint of

Enslow Publishers, Inc.

40 Industrial Road
Box 398
Berkeley Heights, NJ 07922
USA
http://www.enslow.com

E

Earth-Friendly Crafts in **5** Easy Steps

Translated from the Spanish edition by Stacey Juana Pontoriero.
Edited and produced by Enslow Publishers, Inc.

Library of Congress Cataloging-in-Publication Data

Llimós Plomer, Anna.
  [Madera (2007). English]
  Earth-friendly wood crafts in 5 easy steps / Anna Llimós.
    pages cm — (Earth-friendly crafts in 5 easy steps)
  Translation of: Madera / Anna Llimós. — 1a ed. — Barcelona :
  Paramón Paidotribo, 2007.
  Includes bibliographical references and index.
  Summary: "Provides step-by-step instructions on how to create fourteen
simple crafts using wood and cork"—Provided by publisher.
  ISBN 978-0-7660-4193-6
  1. Woodwork—Juvenile literature. 2. Cork craft—Juvenile literature. I. Title.
  TT185.L5613 2013
  684'.08—dc23
                                                    2012013437

Future edition:
Paperback ISBN 978-1-4644-0317-0

Originally published in Spanish under the title *Madera.*
Copyright © 2007 Parramón Paidotribo–World Rights
Published by Parramón Paidotribo, S.L., Badalona, Spain

Production: Sagrafic, S.L.

Text: Anna Llimós

Illustrator: Nos & Soto

Printed in Spain
112012 Indice, S.L., Barcelona, Spain

10 9 8 7 6 5 4 3 2 1

Contents

Puzzle

MATERIALS

6 rectangular pieces of wood
paint–different colors
paintbrush
white glue
1 small cork
1 thumbtack
5 craft sticks
scissors
watercolors
cork sheet

1 Paint hair, a face, and a neck on three different pieces of wood. Let dry.

2 Paint another face and neck on two more pieces of wood. Let dry.

3 For the nose, glue the cork onto one of the faces. Let dry. Stick the thumbtack into the other face to make the other nose.

4

4 Cut the craft sticks into different lengths to make the shirt. Paint them with watercolors. Let dry. Glue them onto a piece of wood below the neck. Let dry.

5 Cut a hat and a shirt from the cork sheet. Glue the hat onto the last blank piece of wood. Glue the shirt onto the other piece of wood below the neck. Let them dry. Move the pieces around to create different characters.

How many different characters can you create?

Rabbit

MATERIALS

1 rectangular piece of wood
paint—different colors
paintbrush
1 clip-style wooden clothespin
wood glue
cork sheet
scissors

1 Paint the rabbit's face onto the piece of wood.

2 Paint the rabbit's body however you wish. Let dry.

3 To make the feet, separate the clothespin into two pieces. Paint them and let them dry.

6

4 Glue the rabbit's body on top of the two clothespin halves. Let dry.

5 Cut two big ears from the cork sheet. Paint them and let them dry. Glue the ears onto the back of the body. Let dry.

I love carrots!

Fly

MATERIALS

2 large corks
1 clip-style wooden clothespin
white glue
masking tape
paint—different colors
paintbrush
cork sheet
scissors

1 Glue the two corks on top of the clothespin. Wrap a piece of masking tape around the corks and clothespin to keep them in place as the glue dries.

2 Remove the masking tape. Paint the cork and clothespin. Let dry.

3 Paint the eyes. Let dry.

8

4 Cut two wings from the cork sheet.

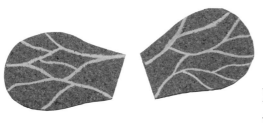

5 Paint the wings any way you like. Let them dry. Glue them to the top of the body and let dry.

Buzz, buzz!

City

MATERIALS

4 pieces of wood of different sizes
paint–different colors
paintbrush
scissors
thin cork sheet
wood glue
thick cork sheet

1 Paint the four pieces of wood as you wish. Let them dry.

2 Paint some windows on one of the pieces of wood. Let dry. Cut a rectangle from the thin cork sheet to make a door. Glue the door onto the piece of wood and let dry.

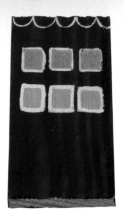

3 Paint windows and a door on another piece of wood. Let dry.

10

4 Paint windows on the third piece of wood and let dry. Cut a round door from the thin cork sheet and glue it on. To make a roof, cut a triangle from the thick cork sheet. Glue it onto the top front edge of the wood. Let dry.

5 Paint balconies and a door on the last piece of wood. Let dry. Place all four of the buildings together.

Build your own city!

Race Cars

MATERIALS

clip-style wooden clothespins
white glue
paint—different colors
paintbrush
cork sheet
scissors

1 Separate a clothespin and glue the two halves together side by side. This will be the race car's body. Let it dry.

2 Paint the race car's body any color you wish. Let dry.

3 Add a number, stripes, or any other decoration you wish.

4 For the wheels, cut four circles from the cork sheet. Paint them black and let dry.

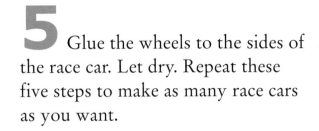

5 Glue the wheels to the sides of the race car. Let dry. Repeat these five steps to make as many race cars as you want.

Vroom, vroom!

Dinosaur

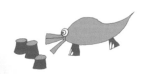

MATERIALS

thick cork sheet
scissors
10 large corks
3 small corks
white glue
3 clip-style wooden clothespins
paint–different colors
paintbrush
thin cork sheet

1 Cut the dinosaur's body from the thick cork sheet.

2 Glue two large corks under the body for the legs. Glue the rest of the large corks along the spine. Glue the three small corks along the tail. Let dry.

3 Paint the three clothespins and the body any color you wish. Let dry.

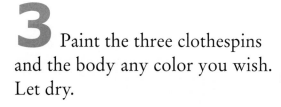

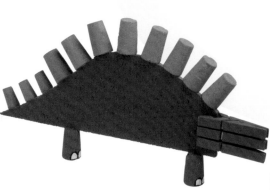

4 To create the head, attach the clothespins to the front end of the body. Paint the toenails and let dry.

5 For the eyes, cut two circles from the thin cork sheet and paint them. Let them dry. Glue one eye to each side of the head. Let dry. Angle the third clothespin downward so it looks like the mouth is open.

A playful dinosaur!

15

Skier

1 large cork
1 medium cork
white glue
paint–different colors
paintbrush
4 toothpicks
2 small corks
1 clip-style wooden clothespin
2 craft sticks
watercolors

1 Glue the medium cork to the large cork. Let dry. This is the head and body.

2 Paint a face, a hat, and the body. Let dry.

3 Paint the toothpicks. These are the arms and legs. Paint the two small corks for boots. Let everything dry.

4 Put some white glue at the ends of the toothpicks. Stick them into the body and the boots.

5 For the skis, separate the clothespin into two pieces and paint them. Paint the two craft sticks with watercolors. Once dry, glue each clothespin half onto a craft stick. Glue the skis to the boots and let dry.

Let's go skiing!

Island

MATERIALS

1 round wooden jar lid
paint-different colors
paintbrush
sponge
toothpicks
white glue
3 large corks
cork sheet
scissors
1 small cork
air-drying clay

1 Paint the center of the jar lid one color and the outside another color. Let dry. Use a sponge lightly dipped in another color to decorate the edge and let dry. If you wish, you may use orange for the island, blue for the ocean, and white for the seafoam.

2 For the palm tree, paint the toothpicks and let them dry. Put some white glue on one end of each toothpick and stick them into a large cork.

3 To finish the palm tree, glue two more large corks to the first one. Once dry, glue the tree onto the island and let that dry.

4 To create the castaway, cut a small strip from the cork sheet. Glue it onto the small cork. Glue a small ball of clay on top of the strip. Let dry.

5 Paint the castaway's face and body and let dry. Glue the castaway to the island. Let dry.

A castaway is stuck on the island.

Bulletin Board

MATERIALS

thick cork sheet
scissors
pencil
1 large rectangular piece of wood
paint—different colors
sponge
paintbrush
white glue
craft drill (Ask an adult for help.)
cord
2 clip-style wooden clothespins
1 small, thin rectangular piece of wood

1 Cut a tree trunk from the cork sheet. Use a pencil to trace its outline onto the large piece of wood.

2 Use a sponge dipped in paint to create the crown of the tree. Use a paintbrush to draw grass and flowers along the bottom of the wood. Once dry, glue the cork tree trunk on top of the outline and let that dry.

3 **Ask an adult** to drill a hole into each top corner of the wood. Pass a cord through the holes and knot the ends so you can hang up your bulletin board.

4 Paint the two clothespins and let them dry. Glue them to the wood. You can use these to hang papers.

5 Paint the small, thin piece of wood. Let dry. Glue it to the larger piece of wood to make a shelf.

Hang your pictures and notes!

Fish

MATERIALS

1 wooden spoon
1 wooden fork
paint-different colors
paintbrush
thin cork sheet
scissors
white glue

1 Paint the wooden spoon and fork any way you wish. Let dry.

2 Paint the eyes and mouth on the wooden spoon. Decorate the fish as you wish. Let dry.

3 Paint eyes and a mouth on the wooden fork. Decorate the body any way you like. Let dry.

4 Cut two pairs of fins from the cork sheet.

5 Paint the fins and let them dry. Glue a pair of fins onto each fish.

Two tropical fish

Acrobat

1 For the arms, separate the clip-type clothespin into two pieces. Glue them to the slotted clothespin.

MATERIALS

1 clip-style wooden clothespin
1 slotted wooden clothespin
(without the metal spring)
white glue
paint–different colors
paintbrush
1 small cork
1 wooden dowel
cord
scissors

2 Paint the body, arms, and legs. Let dry.

3 Paint eyes and a mouth. Let dry.

4 Paint the small cork to make a hat. Once dry, glue it to the head. Paint the wooden dowel. Let dry.

5 Cut two pieces of cord. Tie the acrobat to the dowel.

Hang the acrobat in your room!

Rattle

MATERIALS

1 wooden spatula with holes
paint-different colors
paintbrush
1 craft stick
white glue
raffia
scissors
jingle bells

1 Paint the wooden spatula. Let dry.

2 Decorate the holes as you wish and let dry.

3 Paint the craft stick and let dry.

4 Glue the decorated craft stick onto the spatula's handle. Let dry.

5 Cut several pieces of raffia. Pass a piece through each jingle bell. Tie a jingle bell to each hole in the spatula.

Shake it!

Maze

MATERIALS

1 square piece of wood
paint–different colors
paintbrush
7 craft sticks
scissors
white glue
air-drying clay

1 Paint the piece of wood and let dry.

2 Paint "start" and "end" boxes on opposite corners of the wood. Let dry.

3 Paint one craft stick one color and another craft stick a different color. Let them dry, then cut each one in half. Paint the remaining five craft sticks a third color and let dry.

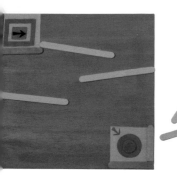

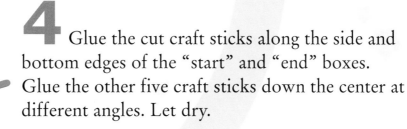

4 Glue the cut craft sticks along the side and bottom edges of the "start" and "end" boxes. Glue the other five craft sticks down the center at different angles. Let dry.

5 Roll a piece of clay into a ball. Let it harden and dry. Now try guiding the ball to the "end" box without allowing it to fall off the wooden tablet.

Play with your friends!

Bird

MATERIALS

1 long piece of wood
2 corks
white glue
1 slotted wooden clothespin
(without the metal spring)
paint-different colors
paintbrush
8 craft sticks
scissors

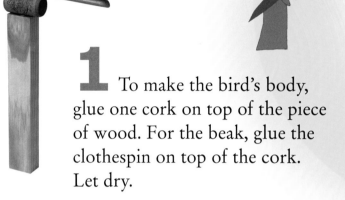

1 To make the bird's body, glue one cork on top of the piece of wood. For the beak, glue the clothespin on top of the cork. Let dry.

2 Paint the body and beak. Let dry.

3 Add details, such as feathers, to the body, if you wish. Paint the eight craft sticks. Let dry.

4 To create the wings, glue four painted craft sticks to each side of the wood. Let dry.

5 Cut two circles from the second cork. Paint them to look like eyes. Glue one to each side of the beak. Let dry.

Such a funny looking bird!

31

Read About

Books

The Bumper Book of Crafty Activities: 100+ Creative Ideas for Kids. Petaluma, Calif.: Search Press, 2012.

Hardy, Emma. *Green Crafts for Children.* New York: Ryland Peters & Small, 2008.

Woodcarving: KidSkills. New York: DK Children, 2009.

Internet Addresses

Kaboose: Wood Crafts
<http://crafts.kaboose.com/wood/index.html>

FamilyFun: Crafts
<http://familyfun.go.com/crafts>

Index
Easy to Hard

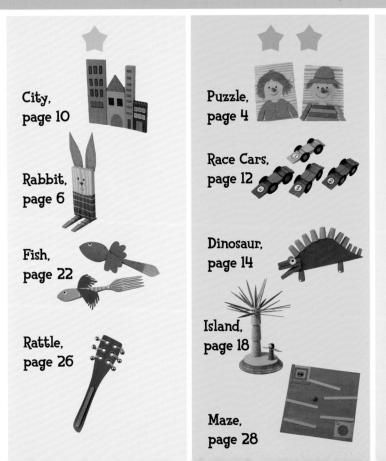
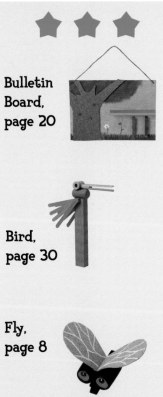